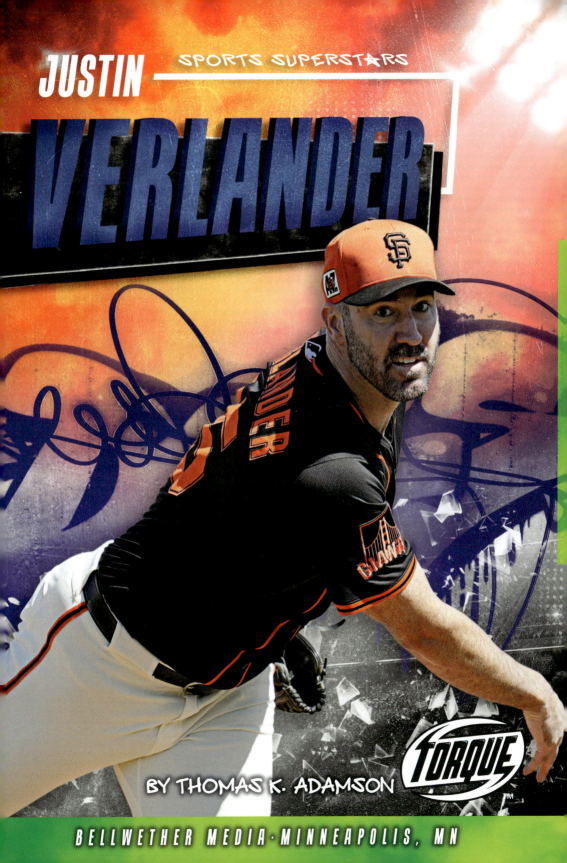

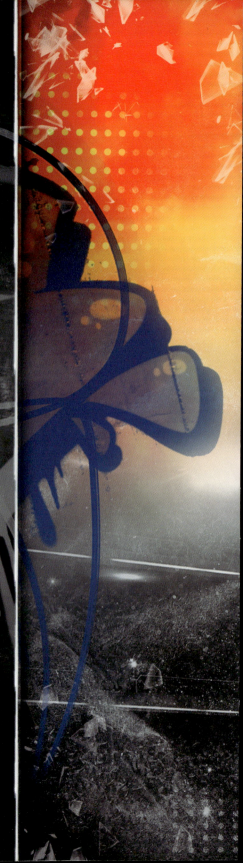

Torque brims with excitement perfect for thrill-seekers of all kinds. Discover daring survival skills, explore uncharted worlds, and marvel at mighty engines and extreme sports. In *Torque* books, anything can happen. Are you ready?

This edition first published in 2026 by Bellwether Media, Inc.

No part of this publication may be reproduced in whole or in part without written permission of the publisher. For information regarding permission, write to Bellwether Media, Inc., Attention: Permissions Department, 3500 American Blvd W, Suite 150, Bloomington, MN 55431.

Library of Congress Cataloging-in-Publication Data

LC record for Justin Verlander available at: https://lccn.loc.gov/2025013769

Text copyright © 2026 by Bellwether Media, Inc. TORQUE and associated logos are trademarks and/or registered trademarks of Bellwether Media, Inc. Bellwether Media is a division of FlutterBee Education Group.

Editor: Kieran Downs   Designer: Gabriel Hilger

Printed in the United States of America, North Mankato, MN.

TABLE OF CONTENTS

GETTING OUT OF A JAM	4
WHO IS JUSTIN VERLANDER?	6
A TALENT FOR PITCHING	8
AWARD-WINNING CAREER	12
VERLANDER'S FUTURE	20
GLOSSARY	22
TO LEARN MORE	23
INDEX	24

GETTING OUT OF A JAM

Game 5 of the 2022 **World Series** is tied. In the 2nd inning, the bases are loaded with two outs. Astros **pitcher** Justin Verlander needs to end the inning.

He throws the next pitch. The batter swings and misses for strike three! The Astros go on to win Game 5. They are one step closer to winning the World Series.

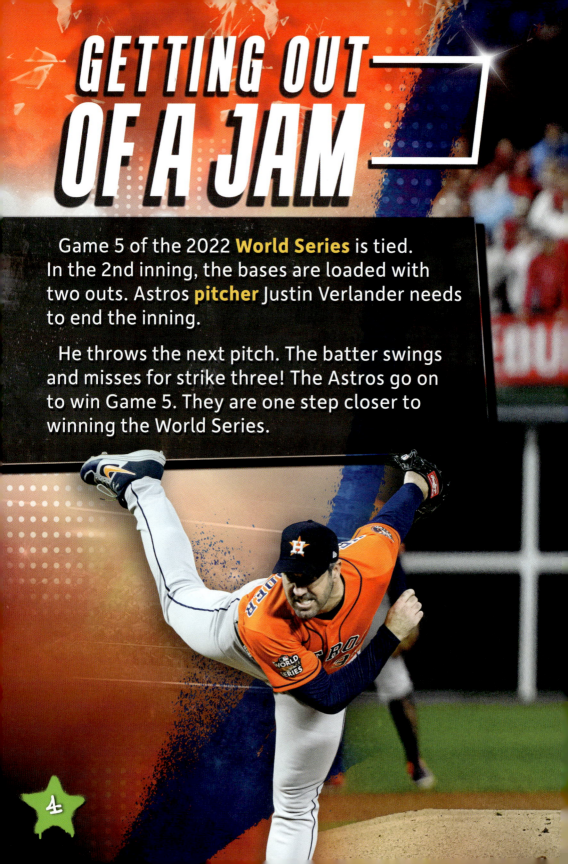

Game Stats

Verlander pitched 5 innings in Game 5. He allowed 1 run and had 6 strikeouts.

WHO IS JUSTIN VERLANDER?

Justin Verlander is a pitcher in **Major League Baseball** (MLB). His **career** has lasted over 20 years. He is considered one of the best pitchers in MLB history.

JUSTIN VERLANDER

BIRTHDAY	February 20, 1983
HOMETOWN	Manakin Sabot, Virginia
POSITION	pitcher
HEIGHT	6 feet 5 inches
DRAFTED	Detroit Tigers in the 1st round (2nd overall) of the 2004 MLB Draft

Verlander is known as a **strikeout** pitcher. In 2024, he moved to 10th on the all-time career strikeout list. He has had a speedy fastball for many years.

7

A TALENT FOR PITCHING

As a kid, Verlander showed baseball talent. His parents and friends noticed his strong arm.

VERLANDER AND HIS PARENTS

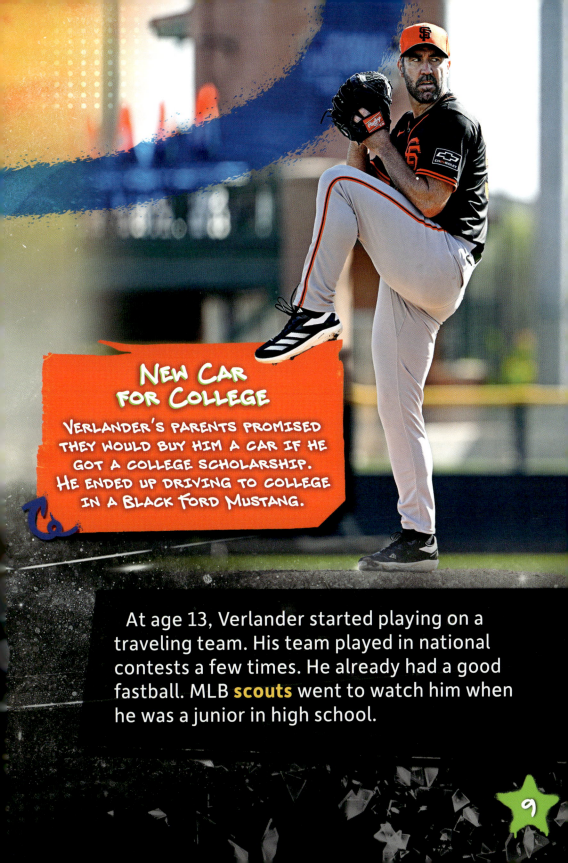

New Car for College

Verlander's parents promised they would buy him a car if he got a college scholarship. He ended up driving to college in a Black Ford Mustang.

At age 13, Verlander started playing on a traveling team. His team played in national contests a few times. He already had a good fastball. MLB **scouts** went to watch him when he was a junior in high school.

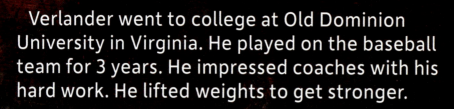

Verlander went to college at Old Dominion University in Virginia. He played on the baseball team for 3 years. He impressed coaches with his hard work. He lifted weights to get stronger.

The Detroit Tigers **drafted** him in the first round in 2004. In 2005, Verlander pitched for **minor league** teams in the Tigers system.

OLD DOMINION UNIVERSITY

College Record-Holder

Verlander holds the Old Dominion record for career strikeouts with 427.

FAVORITES

CANDY	MEAL	PLACE TO TRAVEL	BASEBALL PLAYER AS A KID

Kit Kats	bacon, egg, and cheese sandwich	Italy	Nolan Ryan

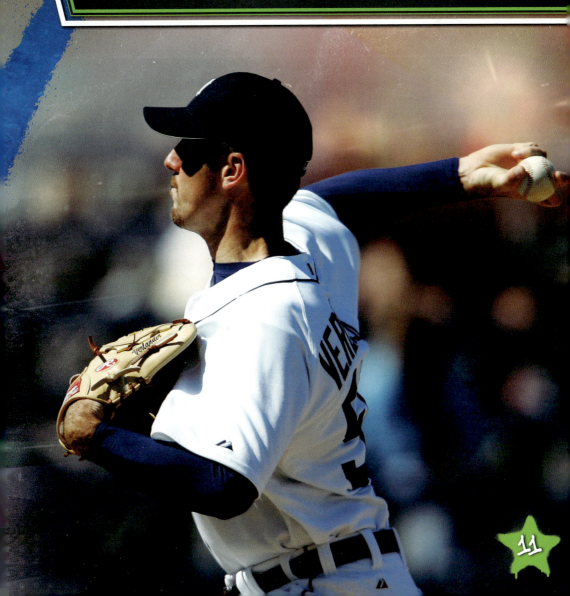

11

AWARD-WINNING CAREER

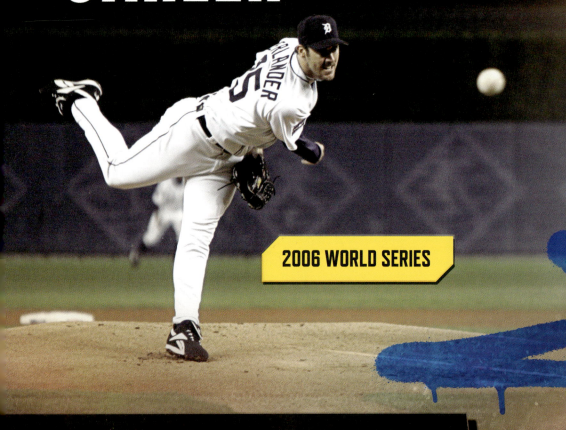

2006 WORLD SERIES

In 2006, Verlander was a big part of a successful Tigers season. He was named the **Rookie** of the Year for the **American League** (AL). He started Game 1 of the 2006 World Series. But the Tigers lost the series.

In 2007, Verlander threw a **no-hitter** in just his second full year. He was named to his first **All-Star Game**.

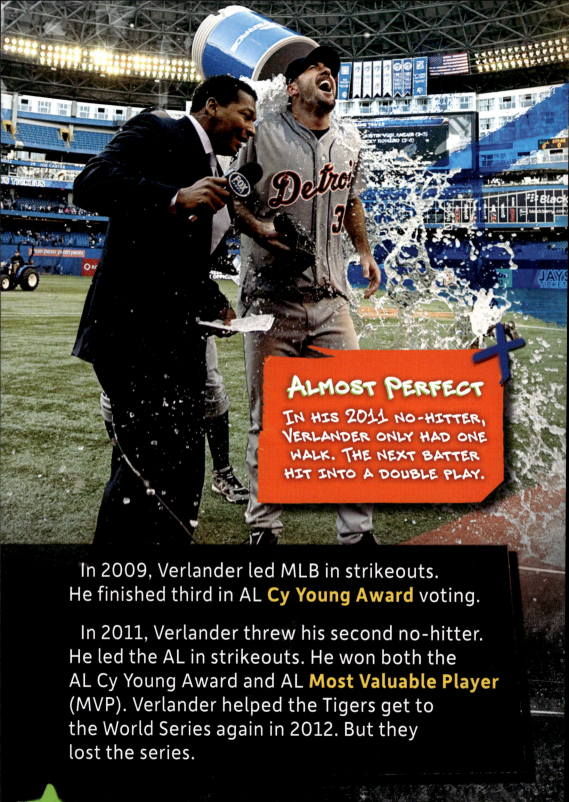

Almost Perfect

In his 2011 no-hitter, Verlander only had one walk. The next batter hit into a double play.

In 2009, Verlander led MLB in strikeouts. He finished third in AL **Cy Young Award** voting.

In 2011, Verlander threw his second no-hitter. He led the AL in strikeouts. He won both the AL Cy Young Award and AL **Most Valuable Player** (MVP). Verlander helped the Tigers get to the World Series again in 2012. But they lost the series.

Verlander finished second in Cy Young voting in 2016. He also recorded his 2,000th strikeout.

The Tigers traded Verlander to the Houston Astros in 2017. He helped the Astros win the World Series. In 2019, he led the Astros to another World Series. But they lost. In 2020, Verlander hurt his throwing elbow. He was out until the 2022 season.

2017 WORLD SERIES

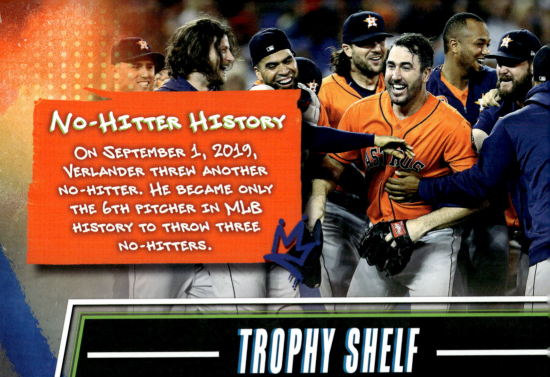

No-Hitter History

On September 1, 2019, Verlander threw another no-hitter. He became only the 6th pitcher in MLB history to throw three no-hitters.

TROPHY SHELF

3-time Cy Young winner

AL MVP

9-time MLB All-Star

AL Rookie of the Year

AL Comeback Player of the Year

2-time World Series Champion

Verlander came back strong in 2022. He helped the Astros win another World Series. He was named the AL Comeback Player of the Year. He also won his third Cy Young Award.

Verlander signed with the New York Mets before the 2023 season. They traded him back to the Astros in August. In 2024 he battled a sore shoulder. In 2025, he signed with the San Francisco Giants.

2022 CY YOUNG AWARD

TIMELINE

— 2004 —
Verlander is drafted by the Tigers

— 2006 —
Verlander is named the AL Rookie of the Year

— 2011 —
Verlander wins the AL MVP and his first Cy Young Award

—2019—
Verlander wins the World Series with the Astros

—2022—
Verlander wins his second World Series

—2025—
Verlander joins the Giants

19

VERLANDER'S FUTURE

Verlander started the Wins for Warriors **Foundation**. This group supports current and former military members and their families.

Verlander keeps throwing strikeouts. He is still climbing the all-time strikeouts list. He is a valuable leader on any team's pitching staff. The long-time expert pitcher wants to win another World Series!

GLOSSARY

All-Star Game—a game between the best players in a league

American League—one of the two major leagues that make up MLB; the other is the National League.

career—the job that a person has for most of their professional life

Cy Young Award—an award given each year to the best pitcher in each major league

drafted—chose to play for a professional team

foundation—an organization that helps people and communities

Major League Baseball—a professional baseball league in the United States; Major League Baseball is often called MLB.

minor league—related to professional baseball leagues below Major League Baseball

most valuable player—the best player in a year, game, or series; the most valuable player is often called the MVP.

no-hitter—a game in which the pitcher does not allow the other team to get a hit for the entire game

pitcher—a player on a baseball team who throws the baseball from the pitcher's mound toward the catcher to begin each play

rookie—a first-year player in a sports league

scouts—people sent to find and bring back information

strikeout—related to an out called in baseball when a batter gets three strikes

World Series—the championship series in Major League Baseball, played between the best team in the American League and the best team in the National League

TO LEARN MORE

AT THE LIBRARY

Downs, Kieran. *Shohei Ohtani*. Minneapolis, Minn.: Bellwether Media, 2023.

Lowe, Alexander. *G.O.A.T. Baseball Pitchers*. Minneapolis, Minn.: Lerner Publications, 2022.

Tischler, Joe. *Houston Astros*. Mankato, Minn.: Creative Education, 2024.

ON THE WEB

FACTSURFER

Factsurfer.com gives you a safe, fun way to find more information.

1. Go to www.factsurfer.com

2. Enter "Justin Verlander" into the search box and click 🔍.

3. Select your book cover to see a list of related content.

INDEX

All-Star Game, 13
American League, 12, 14, 18
awards, 12, 14, 16, 18
childhood, 8, 9
Detroit Tigers, 10, 12, 14, 16
drafted, 10
family, 8, 9
fastball, 7, 9
favorites, 11
Houston Astros, 4, 16, 18
hurt, 16, 18
Major League Baseball, 6, 9, 14, 17
map, 15
minor league, 10
New York Mets, 18
no-hitter, 13, 14, 17
Old Dominion University, 10
outs, 4
pitcher, 4, 6, 7, 17, 21
profile, 7
record, 7, 10, 16, 17, 21
San Francisco Giants, 18
scouts, 9
strike, 4
strikeouts, 5, 7, 10, 14, 16, 21
timeline, 18–19
trophy shelf, 17
Wins for Warriors Foundation, 20
World Series, 4, 5, 12, 14, 15, 16, 18, 21

The images in this book are reproduced through the courtesy of: Ross D. Franklin/ AP Images, front cover; Diamond Images/ Contributor/ Getty Images, p. 3; Chris Szagola/ AP Images, p. 4; Daniel Shirey/ Stringer/ Getty Images, p. 5; Jeff Dean/ Stringer/ Getty Images, p. 6; Andy Kuno/ San Francisco Giants/ Contributor/ Getty Images, pp. 7, 23; Jonathan Daniel/ Staff/ Getty Images, p. 8; Suzanna Mitchell/ San Francisco Giants/ Contributor/ Getty Images, p. 9; Mira/ Alamy Stock Photo, p. 10; Steve Cukrov, p. 11 (kit kat); Adriana, p. 11 (bacon, egg, and cheese sandwich); Yasonya, p. 11 (Italy); Chuck Andersen/ Wikipedia, p. 11 (Nolan Ryan); Matthew Stockman/ Staff/ Getty Images, p. 11 (Justin Verlander); Rich Pilling/ Stringer/ Getty Images, p. 12; Calvin Doctor/ Contributor/ Getty Images, p. 13; Darren Calabrese/ AP Images, p. 14; SNEHIT PHOTO, p. 15 (Detroit Tigers stadium); Another Believer/ Wikipedia, p. 15 (Houston Astros stadium); Wirestock, p. 15 (New York Mets stadium); Marcus Jones, p. 15 (San Francisco Giants stadium); Ron Vesely/ Stringer/ Getty Images, p. 15 (2012 World Series); Ezra Shaw/ Staff/ Getty Images, p. 16; Vaughn Ridley/ Stringer/ Getty Images, p. 17; Mary DeCicco/ Stringer/ Getty Images, p. 18 (2022 Cy Young Award); Detroit Tigers/ Wikipedia, p. 18 (Detroit Tigers logo); Leon Halip/ Contributor/ Getty Images, p. 18 (2006); Dustin Satloff/ Stringer/ Getty Images, p. 19 (Justin Verlander); UPI/ Alamy Stock Photo, p. 19 (2022); San Francisco Giants/ Wikipedia, p. 19 (San Francisco Giants logo); John Parra/ Contributor/ Getty Images, p. 20; Jeff Dean/ Contributor/ Getty Images, p. 21.